DATE DUE

FOLLETT

USA TODAY. **TEEN WISE GUIDES**

A GANNETT COMPANY

TIME, MONEY, AND RELATIONSHIPS

CONFLICT RESOLUTION

SMARTS

How to Communicate, Negotiate, Compromise, and More

MATT DOEDEN

TFCB

TWENTY-FIRST CENTURY BOOKS / MINNEAPOLIS

Twenty-First Century Books
A division of Lerner Publishing Group, Inc.
241 First Avenue North
Minneapolis, MN 55401 U.S.A.

Website address: www.lernerbooks.com

Library of Congress Cataloging-in-Publication Data

Doeden, Matt.
    Conflict resolution smarts : how to communicate, negotiate, compromise, and more / by Matt Doeden.
        p.   cm. — (USA TODAY teen wise guides: time, money, and relationships)
    Includes bibliographical references and index.
    ISBN 978-0-7613-7020-8 (lib. bdg. : alk. paper)
        1. Interpersonal conflict—Juvenile literature. 2. Interpersonal relations—Juvenile literature. 3. Conflict management—Juvenile literature. I. Title.
BF637.I48D64 2012
303.6'9—dc23   2011021555

Manufactured in the United States of America
1 – PP – 12/31/11

CONTENTS

INTRODUCTION
HOPPING MAD!
4

CHAPTER 1
CONFLICT! IT'S NOT A DIRTY WORD
6

CHAPTER 2
HOW TO DEAL: BASIC STRATEGIES
18

CHAPTER 3
TALK IT OUT: CONFLICT AND COMMUNICATION
32

CHAPTER 4
THE FINAL FRONTIER: RESOLUTION
48

EPILOGUE
SUMMING IT UP
58

GLOSSARY   60
SELECTED BIBLIOGRAPHY   61
FOR MORE INFORMATION   62
INDEX   64

HOPPING Mad!

You're so mad, you want to kick something. You feel as if your best friend, Alex, has stabbed you in the back. Every year since you were a kid, you've had all your friends over for a New Year's Eve party. The party is one of your favorite things about the holidays, but you've just heard that Alex is planning a party on the same night. Most of your friends have already agreed to go!

Even best friends can make us angry. Is your disagreement worth ruining a friendship?

You're furious with her. New Year's is *your* event—everyone knows that! But what can you do? You think about putting rotten eggs in her locker or going over to her house to yell and scream. Maybe you could lock yourself in your room and pretend none of this is even happening, or maybe you should just swallow your pride, put on a happy face, and act as if you're not even bothered.

You sit on your bed and take a deep breath. When you think about it, you remember Alex saying something last year about wanting to host the next party, but you just brushed off her comment. A year later, you're hopping mad at your best friend. How are you supposed to deal with it? How can you resolve this conflict without someone getting hurt? *Is there any way to salvage your friendship?*

If you've been in a position like this in real life, keep reading. This book will give you tools for dealing with conflict. Maybe there's still hope for your party *and* your friendship.

1 CONFLICT! IT'S NOT *a Dirty Word*

People often bring conflicts into the public arena. They protest, hoping to bring attention to their point of view. The protesters on the left are fighting for the right for same-sex couples to legally marry. The protesters on the right believe that marriage should only be allowed between a man and a woman.

Conflict is a pretty broad term. It can mean anything from an all-out war between nations to a squabble between toddlers over a toy. Basically, a conflict is a disagreement between two or more people or groups. Each side of a conflict has different goals and wants a different outcome.

You might think of conflict as a negative thing, as something to be avoided. After all, conflict can be unpleasant, uncomfortable, and stressful. Arguments can damage and sometimes end friendships, marriages, and other relationships. In politics, conflict can cause gridlock, a situation in which nothing gets done because neither side is willing to compromise. When conflict leads to war, hundreds of thousands of people might get killed.

INTERNAL CONFLICT

Can you have conflict with nobody but yourself? Sure! A person can be conflicted by clashing internal thoughts or belief systems. Maybe you have a chance to cheat on a test in school. You desperately need a good grade, but you just can't grasp the material. A part of you *wants* to cheat, another part of you believes that cheating is wrong, and yet another part is afraid of getting caught. In this situation, your thoughts and beliefs are in conflict with one another, and you have to be the final judge and jury in resolving the conflict. Only you can decide which thoughts to listen to and which to tune out.

But conflict doesn't always have to be negative. Players on a basketball team might have conflicting ideas about how to run an offense. But if the players get together and figure out which ideas are best, the whole team can improve its play. Similarly, politicians with different ideas can blend the best ones to create new laws. Handled properly, conflict can be a positive thing, with results that benefit everyone. Handling conflict in a positive way is called conflict management, and bringing a conflict to a conclusion is called conflict resolution.

THE ROOT OF IT ALL

It's no secret that everyone experiences conflict. Your parents, your friends—heck, even your dog gets its share! But what causes conflict? Why do we constantly find ourselves at odds with others? Conflict can arise for countless reasons, but most conflicts come down to a few root causes.

COMPETITION

Competition can be a lot of fun. Whether you like to compete in sports, math leagues, video games, or for the best grades in class, the thrill of going up against others can be a real rush. But competition also causes conflict. When two or more people compete, they are working toward incompatible goals. Sports are a great example of competition. In a football game, the competition is clear-cut. The offense wants to move the ball and score points, and the defense wants to stop the offense. So the two sides have opposite goals, and only one side will get what it wants. One side will meet its goals, while the other will fail.

But competition isn't limited to sports and games. *Anywhere people want the same limited resource, conflict can arise.* Two boys might want to take the same girl to the prom, two girls might compete for the same spot in the school band, or two nations might compete over disputed territory. In these situations, one side will win and the other will lose, much as with the offense and defense in a football game.

Competition is a form of conflict. In most games, one side will win, while the other will lose. One team will be disappointed.

Conflict between teens and their parents is common.

DIFFERING VALUES OR BELIEFS

It's probably safe to bet that you and your parents don't always see eye to eye. They might think nine in the evening is a perfectly reasonable time for your weekend curfew, while that same time might seem ridiculous to you. This is a simple case of two people or groups holding different points of view. From your parents' point of view, letting you stay out late is just inviting trouble—the kind of trouble teenagers can find after the sun goes down. But from your point of view, you're missing out on all the fun your friends will have after you go home. You and your parents are using different experiences and beliefs to form an opinion. When those opinions clash, presto! *You get conflict.*

No two people have identical life experiences and ideas, so we're constantly running into differences of opinion. Men and women often see things differently. So do young people and older people or people from different cultures or religions.

POOR COMMUNICATION

Some conflicts arise out of simple misunderstandings or poor communication. Maybe you've noticed that a friend has dropped a lot of weight in recent months. You might say to him, "Wow, you're looking good. You must have started exercising." You mean the comment as a compliment, but your friend takes it to mean that you thought he used to be overweight and lazy. This is a classic case of miscommunication. The message you meant to send wasn't the message the other person received. When miscommunication happens, all sorts of mayhem can result.

With poor communication, two people who actually agree on a topic might not even realize it. They might find themselves in a conflict that was never even necessary. Imagine that you and a classmate are preparing a presentation for history class. Your classmate insists on starting the presentation with a joke, but you want to stick to the facts. You butt heads over the issue for half an hour before you realize that your classmate's joke is actually *about* the facts. It's not just some random, tasteless joke. In this case, you failed to communicate effectively and were dragged through a pointless argument.

THE STAGES OF CONFLICT

Most conflicts don't just suddenly happen. They build up over time and go through some basic stages as they evolve. Understanding the stages of conflict can help you manage them.

DEALING
WITH DIVERSITY

A big part of managing conflict is understanding that different people have different points of view. People from different races, religions, and cultural backgrounds might have different values and ideas. Understanding that people with different backgrounds might think differently than you do is an important part of conflict management.

Imagine a few examples. A teenager who lives on a farm might not think twice about slaughtering an animal for food. But a city teen, who gets food only from the supermarket and restaurants, might find this idea horrifying. A kid from a religious home might not like to hear someone swearing, while someone from a less religious family might feel that words are just words. The kids' different backgrounds give them very different ideas about what is offensive and what is not. You don't have to agree with the values and beliefs of others, but if you can *understand* them, it will go a long way toward making conflict management easier and more productive.

Think of a conflict as a seed. At first, the seed is buried beneath the ground, and it's possible that nobody even knows it's there. If the conditions are right, the little seed of a conflict might begin to grow. It can put down strong roots before it ever breaks the surface. Maybe you and a friend are trying out for the same part in a school play, but neither of you knows that the other is interested in the part. The seed of conflict is planted, even if neither of you can see it yet.

Next comes a triggering event—an event that makes one person aware of the conflict. Maybe you overhear your friend reciting lines, practicing to try out for the same part you want. All at once, you realize she's after the part, and you feel a twinge of anger or hurt feelings. The conflict is not a seed anymore. It's become a plant that has sent shoots up through the ground, where everyone can see them.

Once both you and your friend become aware of the situation, you're in a full-fledged conflict. It's time to manage that conflict. If you don't, it's going to grow and grow like a weed. Maybe one of you will decide to try out for a different part in the play, so you don't have to compete with a friend. Or maybe your friend will end up getting the part, but you'll acknowledge that she did the best job at tryouts and really deserved the part, so you'll cheer her on. It could even be that neither one of you gets a part in the play. Whatever ends up happening, the conflict will be resolved in one way or another.

Conflict could arise if two friends try out for the same part in a school play.

BOILING UP WITH ANGER
AMERICANS SEEM MAD A LOT: IS STRESS OR THE INTERNET TO BLAME?

By Sharon Jayson

Are we bad for getting mad? Psychologists say it's normal to get angry. We all do it— and we need to feel anger. It's a basic human emotion, they say.

More and more, though, we see people losing their cool in public. And the kind of outbursts seen at town hall meetings on health care reform, on tennis courts, on the Internet and even during speeches by the president are increasingly a part of everyday life.

There's no official data suggesting Americans are angrier today than in the past. Psychologists and other experts even disagree on whether people really are angrier or just have fewer inhibitions [hesitations] about acting out in public. Some say narcissism [self-centeredness] and feelings of entitlement [a belief that one is deserving of certain privileges], which are reportedly on the rise, make people upset when they don't get what they want. And the culture of open expression—including TV and radio talk shows that fuel the fury— suggests that explosive behavior is becoming routine.

There are plenty of things to be angry about lately: lost jobs, pay cuts, reduced home values and war, to name just a few. "You see pictures on the news of these grown adults screaming and yelling at each other over the whole [health] insurance issue," says workshop leader John Lee of Mentone, Alabama, author of *The Anger Solution*, published in September. "When there's a massive amount of stress, there will be massive amounts of anger and rage."

"Anger is a normal, natural, emotional experience that is characteristic not only of people but of animals," says Charles Spielberger, director of the Center for Research in Behavioral Medicine and Health Psychology at the University of South Florida-Tampa. Spielberger, a psychologist known for developing a widely used system to measure people's anger, says anger is "built into us" and has helped humans survive. "Anger signals a need that is not being filled.

There's nothing wrong with anger," says Robert Allan, a clinical psychologist at Weill Cornell Medical College/New York Presbyterian Hospital in New York. "The question is how you express it."

On the plus side, anger can bring about change. Think about the American Revolution, the Boston Tea Party, women's suffrage [voting rights], the civil rights movement. "Good anger can get you motivated to resolve conflicts and to fix social injustice and to overcome obstacles in your life," DiGiuseppe says. "You would never want to eliminate" all anger.

In the workplace, anger also can motivate employees, as long as it's not expressed in a shouting match or fisticuffs [a fight with fists], says Ricky Griffin, a professor of management at Texas A&M University-College Station, who studies workplace aggression. "If my boss gives me a low performance appraisal, I may get angry about it, but it may make me want to prove my boss is wrong by working harder," he says.

But if hostility or rage takes over, employer responses can range from not promoting the employee to firing the worker. For real anger issues, many people look to anger management to help handle their feelings. Spielberger says the first step in dealing with angry feelings is to recognize them. "The next step is to try to understand the circumstances that have evoked those feelings. Then you need to look at expressing the anger in ways that will deal with the problem instead of ways that can injure other people."

The most important thing to understand about anger is "if you have too much of it, you can learn to manage it," Allan says. "You need to prioritize and ask yourself how important it is before you make an issue of something."

—*November 19, 2009*

EVERYONE RESPONDS DIFFERENTLY

Everyone responds differently to conflict, and some reactions work better than others. Imagine a group of boys sitting around playing video games. One guy wants to play a shooting game, someone else wants to play a football game, and a third player wants to try the latest, greatest racing game. What do they do?

Suppose one of the kids isn't willing to talk about it. He just grabs all the controllers and insists on getting his way. This guy is dominating the conflict.

Another person might prefer to avoid or ignore the conflict. Maybe the guy who wants to play the shooting game just gets up and leaves. He'd rather not play at all than deal with the conflict. For him, not getting his way is worth not having to take part in the argument.

The third guy responds to conflict in a different way—he doesn't try to dominate it or avoid it. Instead, he

USA TODAY Snapshots®

Weighing heavily on kids

Asked to rate 20 health issues facing children in their communities, adults said the biggest problems are:

Obesity	35%
Drug abuse	33%
Smoking/ Tobacco use	32%
Bullying	28%
Internet safety	27%

Source:
Knowledge Networks survey of 2,064 adults ages 18 and older for the C.S. Mott Children's Hospital National Poll on Children's Health

By Michelle Healy and Sam Ward, USA TODAY, 2008

Modern kids face a lot of pressures, including bullying. Even the Internet can be a source of conflict. You can use your conflict resolution skills to make your teen years less stressful.

tries to manage it. He's most interested in coming to an agreement that everyone can be happy with. He might suggest that the group spend a half hour playing each game. This guy is not trying to get his own way but is trying to find a solution that everyone can agree on. Sounds like a useful guy to have around, doesn't it?

In the long run, trying to solve conflicts is generally the best strategy. You won't always be able to come up with a solution that everyone likes, but trying to understand the goals of every side and doing what you can to make a fair agreement is a key to good conflict management.

Conflict can spring up at any time. Even a group of friends hanging out playing video games might disagree on how to spend their time.

2 HOW TO DEAL:
Basic Strategies

Learning how to handle conflicts with
others is an important life skill.

Conflict is nothing new. It's been around since the dawn of time, and it's not even unique to people. Imagine a lion hunting a gazelle on the plains of Africa. This is a conflict. The lion's goal is to eat the gazelle, and the gazelle's goal is to not be eaten by the lion. Goals don't get much more opposite and incompatible than that!

All right, maybe there's not a lot of room for conflict management between a lion and a gazelle. But people are different. We can think, reason, and communicate. We are capable of empathy—the ability to understand the thoughts and feelings of others. Our rational minds are able to come up with ways to resolve our differences.

Experts have identified a few basic strategies for managing and resolving conflict. These strategies are competition, compromise, accommodation, arbitration, mediation, and collaboration.

In a tennis match, each side is playing to win.

COMPETITION—
WINNER TAKES ALL

There's that word again: *competition*. In chapter 1, we discussed competition as a cause of conflict, but competition is also a way to *resolve* conflict. Competition is a winner-takes-all strategy in conflict management. One side gets exactly what it wants, while the other side doesn't get any of what it wants. You end up with a clear-cut winner and a clear-cut loser.

Competition may sound like a bad way to resolve conflicts—but actually, it's not. Every toddler learns that sometimes you just can't get your way, and competition is a straightforward way to decide when you do and when you don't. Once again, we can look at sports as an example.

In tennis, each player's goal is to win the match. The two players can't both get what they want, so they play the game. They compete against each other. In the end, somebody wins and somebody loses.

Competition can work well in many situations besides sporting events. Suppose two students are competing for the title of class valedictorian. Only the student with the higher grade-point average will get the honor, so the two students compete directly with each other. Both of them strive to do their best. One of them will "win," while the other will "lose"—but the outcome will still be positive. By competing, the two students push themselves to excel at their schoolwork.

Competition as a method of conflict resolution has its place, but often it's not the best choice. Nobody likes to lose, and many conflicts aren't easily resolved by head-to-head competition.

When students compete for the best grades or test scores, the result can be positive. Everyone improves academically.

GIVE AND TAKE: COMPROMISE

If a winner-takes-all strategy doesn't sound like a bed of roses to you, don't worry. You can use other methods to tackle life's conflicts. Compromise is a good choice.

You probably make compromises every day without thinking much about it. Maybe your mom wants you to work on your history paper, but you want to watch TV. You might agree to watch thirty minutes of TV and then start on the paper. Or you might agree that once you finish the paper, you can watch TV all you want. With this strategy, you consider the goals of both parties and come up with a solution that satisfies everyone. That's compromise in a nutshell.

Negotiation is often a part of compromise. When you negotiate, you're trying to get as much of what you want as you can. Suppose you're ready to go out and buy your first car. You head over to the local used car dealer with your checkbook in hand. You find a sweet ride, but the price tag is a bit more than you want to spend. You start to negotiate the price with a salesperson at the dealership. You make an offer, and she counters with a higher price. Both sides want the same thing— for you to drive away with the car—but you each try to get as much out of the deal as you can. You go back and forth, making offers and counteroffers until you either agree on a price or walk away with no deal.

Many businesses encourage you to negotiate over price. At a used car lot, the price on the windshield is usually just a starting point for negotiations.

WE'RE ON STRIKE!

Have you ever seen news coverage of a strike? You might have seen people marching in long lines, chanting, and holding signs. Workers sometimes go on strike when they're unhappy with their pay or working conditions. They refuse to do their jobs, bringing the employer's business—and profits—to a halt. The workers ask for certain improvements, such as higher pay, and they vow not to return to work until their demands are met. In most strikes, the two sides end up negotiating. The workers might ask for a certain pay raise, the employer might counteroffer, and so on until the two sides meet in the middle.

These members of the Writers Guild of America strike in December 2007. They protested the inequality of pay for writers compared with the huge profits made by movie and television studios.

Sometimes when two people want the same thing, neither of them gets what she wants.

NOT WORTH THE FIGHT: ACCOMMODATION

Imagine you're at the mall with a friend. You're browsing through a store when you both spot a pair of sunglasses on sale. They're dirt cheap, and they look fantastic. You both want the sunglasses, but there's a problem: the store has only the one pair left.

What do you do? You could compete for the glasses—each grabbing for them, with the "winner" getting to buy them, but that's not a very civilized solution. And there's really no room for compromise in this situation—you can't both buy the glasses.

Welcome to Accommodation 101. One of you has to step aside and let the other get his or her way. Perhaps you value your friendship and don't want something silly like a pair of sunglasses to come between you, or maybe your friend knows that you've had a bad week and thinks you need a boost. Even though both of you want the glasses, one of you decides to accommodate, or give in. *Like competition, accommodation is a win-lose strategy, but it's one that the "losing" person willingly accepts.*

Just giving up may not sound like much of a strategy, but you might use accommodation more often that you realize. Making and keeping friends often requires a healthy dose of accommodation. This strategy is usually best for small and generally unimportant conflicts. For instance, if you and a friend are standing in line at the movie theater and disagree about which movie to see, somebody has to accommodate. As much as you might want to see the latest sci-fi thriller, it's not something your life depends on, so you agree to go with your friend's pick.

But be sure you're not always the one stepping aside, and you shouldn't resort to accommodation for truly important things. Suppose a friend wants to go to a party where kids will be drinking and taking drugs, and you think that's a bad call. This is a time to dig your heels in and stand up for yourself. The trick with accommodation is to know which battles are worth fighting.

USA TODAY Snapshots®

Early on, social skills trump smarts
Percentage of 800 kindergarten teachers surveyed who say these skills are essential or very important:

Paying attention — 86%
Not being disruptive — 86%
Following directions — 83%
Getting along with others — 83%
Problem-solving — 61%
Knowing the alphabet — 32%
Counting to 20 — 27%

Source: Mason-Dixon Polling for Fight Crime: Invest in Kids
By Julia Neyman and Alejandro Gonzalez, USA TODAY, 2004

Conflict resolution skills start young. Even kindergartners need to get along well with others.

A LITTLE HELP:
ARBITRATION AND MEDIATION

Sometimes you'll run into a conflict that you can't seem to resolve. You can't compete over it, neither party is willing to accommodate, and you can't reach a compromise. What next?

It might be time to bring in a neutral third person to help find a solution. This process is called arbitration or mediation. In mediation, someone simply helps the two sides negotiate. This third person—the mediator—doesn't decide the outcome of the conflict. He or she just helps both sides come to an agreement. Mediation is a bit like compromise but with some help. Arbitration is similar to mediation. Once again, a third person listens to both sides of the conflict. But in arbitration, this person gets to decide how the conflict will be resolved. Both sides agree beforehand to honor whatever decision the arbitrator reaches.

People often use mediation and arbitration in legal disputes, such as divorces. Sometimes workers and employers use mediation or arbitration to come to agreements about wages, employment benefits (such as health insurance or vacation time), and work hours. But these processes don't have to be formal. *At some high schools, students serve as mediators to help resolve conflicts between fellow students.*

Mediation and arbitration aren't always perfect. Think back to when you were small. Did you ever get into a fight with a sibling or another child and then run to a parent to tattle? A child running to a parent or other adult is looking for someone to step in and solve the problem. Although you didn't know the words at the time, you were really looking for a mediator or an arbitrator.

Of course, if you squint your eyes and think really hard, you might also remember being scolded and told that nobody likes a tattletale. Or maybe the adult just sighed and told you and the other child to work things out yourselves. Why did the adult do that? He or she knew that it's usually better if people can work out problems on their own. The adult wanted you to build your own conflict management skills, knowing that these skills would be important as you got older. After all, you can't always rely on somebody else to solve your problems. That's why arbitration and mediation should be a last resort.

Sometimes people need help settling a disagreement. In these cases, they may ask a third party to help resolve their conflict.

USA TODAY
Life
SECTION D
LIFE.USATODAY.COM

STUDENTS RALLY TODAY
FOR QUALITY EDUCATION

By Mary Beth Marklein

College students on more than 100 campuses nationwide plan walkouts, rallies and other actions today to protest budget cuts, layoffs and tuition increases, which they say erode quality of education and limit access. Students in at least 32 states are expected to join the campaign. It has been bubbling up since demonstrations last fall in California, where students, faculty and unions [groups of workers] protested plans for a 32% tuition increase amid the state's fiscal crisis. "Students saw that there was an opportunity to do something in their own states because the budget cuts didn't happen just in California," says Monique Teal of the United States Student Association, which represents student governments.

These University of California students took their conflict with state government to the streets. They were unhappy with budget cuts and tuition increases.

University of California [UC] regents [the school's governing body] increased fees as planned. But Gov. Arnold Schwarzenegger has proposed that at least 10% of annual state spending go to the UC and California State University systems.

Most of today's efforts focus on public education, where enrollments are growing most rapidly and tuition has risen fastest. But some private schools, including the University of Chicago and Eckerd College in St. Petersburg, Florida, are protesting the effects of campus budget cuts. "The biggest thread that ties these protests together is the current financial crisis in higher education," says Angus Johnston, who teaches history at City University of New York and tracks protests on his blog, studentactivism.net.

"We're seeing more classes taught by [people] who aren't getting paid [fairly]. We're seeing larger class sizes, and some kids in certain majors can't get all the courses they need in four years," says Maryland junior Jon Berger.

California State University chancellor Charles Reed says federal stimulus money kept the effect of budget cuts on his 23-campus system to a minimum. But "students are paying more and getting less, and they have every right to be outraged about that."

—*March 4, 2010*

THE ULTIMATE SOLUTION:
COLLABORATION

Maybe you're noticing a pattern here. When you use any of the strategies discussed above, somebody has to give. Either one person "loses" or both people have to give up something to reach a solution. But wouldn't it be great if everyone could come away from the conflict completely happy? It's possible. *The ultimate conflict management strategy is collaboration.* With successful collaboration, everyone walks away happy.

Suppose you and some friends want to go out for lunch. A few of you are craving pizza, but one of your friends can't eat cheese without getting sick. Another friend is desperate for Chinese food, and a third has a hankering for a burger. Some of you could accommodate by giving up on what you want, or you could all compromise and go out for tacos instead. But with these solutions, not everybody is 100 percent happy. Wait a minute! You remember that the local mall has a food court. There, you can all eat together, and everyone can eat what he or she wants. You've collaborated and found a solution in which everybody wins.

If you can work together to find a solution that makes everyone happy, everyone wins.

BE A PEER MEDIATOR

At many schools, students help resolve conflicts between their peers, or fellow classmates. These students take special training to become mediators. Peer mediators don't decide how to resolve conflicts, and they don't have power to enforce decisions. Instead, their job is to help the parties communicate and come to their own conflict resolutions. Many students say that it's easier to resolve problems with a peer mediator than with a teacher or other adult acting as a mediator.

Peer mediation has proved useful in resolving conflicts over gossip, bullying, racial confrontations, and other relationship difficulties. If you're interested in peer mediation, talk to a teacher or principal. Your school might already have a program, or your suggestion might encourage the school staff to start one.

Fifth grader Marisa Garcia shakes hands with Judge Emily Mueller. Garcia was sworn in as peer mediator of West Ridge Elementary School in Racine, Wisconsin.

3 TALK IT OUT: CONFLICT AND *Communication*

Communication is the key to resolving conflict. Make sure to hear each other out before you decide on the best solution.

Whenever you find yourself in a conflict, the first thing to do is communicate. You won't find a solution until you know exactly what the conflict is and where it's coming from. And don't just assume you know! Someone else might see a situation completely differently than you do, and you won't know that unless you talk. By communicating, you can discover what the other person wants and why he or she wants it. At the same time, you can express your own thoughts and goals. Only when you fully understand both sides of the conflict will you be able to decide which strategy works best.

Maybe your sister is angry at you for borrowing her MP3 player. By talking to her, you might discover that she doesn't really care if you use it—she's just mad that you never put it back on the charger when you're done. In this case, the solution is easy: you promise to put the MP3 player back on the charger when you're done using it, and everyone's happy. Of course, not all conflicts will be so easy to resolve, but you won't know unless you communicate.

BEWARE OF GHOSTS!

Dudley Weeks, an author and professor of conflict resolution, warns people to watch out for "ghost conflicts." A ghost conflict is a minor or trivial conflict that people focus on to avoid dealing with more serious issues. For example, a girl and her parents might choose to ignore an important issue, such as the daughter's poor grades at school. They may instead argue over a ghost conflict, such as whether the daughter can get a tattoo.

Ghost conflicts can quickly grow out of control because the people involved aren't talking about the real issues. By seeing through the ghosts, people can get down to what matters and start working on problems that truly need solving.

CHECK YOUR EMOTIONS

It's easy to get emotional during a conflict, but too much emotion can be a roadblock to reaching a solution. Feelings such as fear, anger, and helplessness can cloud a person's ability to think rationally. Getting control of your own emotions and understanding the emotions of others can go a long way toward reaching a solution.

TIME-OUT

Try to calm yourself before talking about a conflict. If the conversation becomes too heated and feels out of control, take a time-out. This cooling-off period is critical for making sure that the conflict doesn't escalate and turn into violence.

If calming down is a challenge, try some basic relaxation techniques. Close your eyes, take a deep breath through your nose, and then exhale slowly through your mouth. Concentrate on the process of breathing. This exercise will help slow your heartbeat and hopefully settle your mind.

Or you can try some simple meditation. Close your eyes and imagine yourself in a place where you feel safe. Build the place in your mind, imagining the sounds, smells, and sights there. Spend a few imaginary moments in this place. This too will help bring you to a calmer, more rational state of mind. Then you'll be much better prepared to do some serious conflict management.

It's best to approach a conflict with a calm state of mind. Meditation and deep breathing can help you relax.

35

When talking over a conflict, try to remain calm. Yelling will only make the situation worse.

CHOOSING YOUR WORDS

You can't control the emotions of others, but what you say *can* affect them. Words are powerful, and choosing yours carefully is a critical part of managing a conflict.

Talking about a conflict can be stressful for everyone. Hard feelings can turn into harsh words, only making matters worse. *It doesn't do any good to talk about a conflict unless you can do it in a civil, productive manner.* Remember, you're talking in hopes of making things better, not worse. You don't want conflict escalating into confrontation and violence. Instead, you want to keep emotions low and level. You want to be calm, rational, and logical. How do you make that happen?

Although *what* you say is important, *how* you say it is almost as important. If you start firing off accusations, the other person in the discussion probably won't be receptive to you. So you'll need a different approach.

Many experts in conflict management suggest using statements that begin with the pronoun *I*. These statements are usually less emotionally charged than those that start with *you*. Imagine that your friend Lindsey just unfriended you on Facebook. When you talk to her about it, you could say, "You hurt me," or you could say, "I was hurt that you didn't want me on your friends list anymore." See the difference? The first statement could sound like an accusation or an attack to Lindsey, and she might not be willing to discuss the situation if she feels attacked. In the second statement, you're explaining your feelings, not accusing her of anything. Lindsey is more likely to be receptive to this statement.

Then flip the script. If Lindsey were to respond, "You wouldn't stop making stupid posts on my page," that might sting a little. But if Lindsey instead said, "I felt that my page was getting too cluttered by your posts. Remember, I asked you not to post so much there," you might not feel so hurt. Both statements send the same message, but the "I statement" doesn't come across as strong. Using "I statements" is a simple way to get better results.

When discussing a conflict, use "I statements" instead of "you statements." Explain your feelings without labeling or accusing the other person.

CAUGHT IN THE CATTY CORNER;
EXPERTS CALL IT "RELATIONAL AGGRESSION,"
BUT ADOLESCENT GIRLS SAY PEERS ARE JUST MEAN

By Nanci Hellmich

Katy's seventh-grade year was a girl's worst nightmare. She was excluded from parties, lunch table groups, conversations and cliques. She was teased and taunted about her looks and her glasses. She was treated this way by "the meanest people I ever met, and they were all girls," says Katy. "There was a lot of plotting and scheming behind people's backs. It was horrible. I don't remember anything I learned that year."

But there was a silver lining: She met her best friend during that trying time. "We do almost everything together. She's always there for me," says Katy, now 17.

Katy's experience mirrors that of millions of girls across the country as they make their way through the often painful passage of adolescence. Out of this pain often comes strength of character and genuine friendships, but while it's happening, a girl's life can be total misery. Now, some behavior experts are doing research to try to understand this phenomenon. And while they realize they may not be able to—and perhaps shouldn't—totally change it, there may be ways to help girls get through it with fewer scars.

[Psychology professor Sharon] Lamb believes girls would have less aggression with other girls if they learned to be more straightforward and honest about their feelings. "In all relationships, if you get angry with people, you talk it out," she says. She recommends that parents teach their girls how to handle confrontation with dignity. They need to teach them to stand up against injustice for other people and for themselves.

Parents can help by giving their daughter the words to express her feelings. For example, if their daughter is teased about her clothes, the parents might suggest she say, "What you are doing is hurtful, and there is no good reason to treat me this way because clothes really don't matter." Even if the daughter doesn't say the words to her tormenter, she can rehearse them in her mind and find comfort in them, Lamb says.

Parents also need to be good listeners and guide their children without telling them what to do, Rubin says. Parents should be a big ear, not a commandant, he says. For example, if a girl says she wants to be friends with a girl who is shunning her, then the parent might ask: "Why do you want to be friends with her? What would you get out of the relationship? Is there anybody else in school whom you might be interested in being friends with?"

Clinical psychologist Roni Cohen-Sandler, author of *Trust Me, Mom—Everyone Else Is Going!* says kids can learn lifelong lessons in these experiences. They need to know there is meanness in the world, and they need to figure out how they are going to deal with it, she says. This prepares them for jobs where they'll confront people who are "nice and collaborative, and people who are mean and jockey for power."

When Katy was suffering through friendship traumas, her parents were always there for her and willing to listen, she says. One of the most valuable lessons she has learned from her experiences is the hurtfulness of gossiping and meanness. "I catch myself when I want to say something mean, and I stop because I know what it feels like to be on the other side."

—*April 9, 2002*

USA TODAY Snapshots®

Scared at school

Percentage of students ages 12-18 who were bullied at school during the previous six months, by location of bullying:

Inside school **79%**

Outside on school grounds **28%**

School bus **8%**

Somewhere else **5%**

Source: Department of Education

By David Stuckey and Alejandro Gonzalez, USA TODAY, 2006

Conflicts at school can take many forms, but bullying is common. Experts say that kids can use conflict resolution skills to stand up to bullies and to sort out hurt feelings.

LISTEN UP!

Communication is a two-way street. It isn't just about talking. In conflict management, you're not just there to tell your side of the story. If communication is going to work, you also have to be a good listener. In fact, listening to the other person might be even more important than telling your side of the story.

Nobody likes to be ignored. If a friend or a family member completely disregarded your feelings, you'd be hurt, right? So don't disregard his or her feelings either. Even if the other person is saying things you don't want to hear or things you disagree with, listen patiently. You don't have to agree, but you should let the person know that you're listening. Don't roll your eyes or look impatient. Be attentive and polite. If you disagree, you can use phrases such as, "I understand what you're telling me, even if I don't agree with it."

LAYING DOWN THE LAW

Often it makes sense to agree to some ground rules before discussing a conflict. Following these rules will make your communication much more effective:

- No name-calling. Insults can quickly cause an otherwise rational discussion to flare up into an argument. Make all name-calling off-limits.
- No interrupting. Nobody likes to be cut off in the middle of a thought. Agree that the speaker has a right to finish what he or she is saying. Guarantee that all parties will get a chance to speak—they just have to do it in turn.
- No shouting. Agree to keep your voices calm and level. Shouting causes emotions to stir and gets in the way of progress.

Conflicts with family members can be more emotionally charged than conflicts with friends or strangers.

COMMUNICATING AT HOME

Managing conflicts with friends and classmates is one thing, but dealing with family members can be a whole different ball game. Maybe you find yourself constantly fighting with a brother or a sister or frequently butting heads with one or both of your parents. Or maybe your parents are always fighting and dragging you into the middle of it.

Communicating with family members is often more complicated than talking with strangers. Even when you're boiling mad at a family member, you probably still love that person. He or she is still family, right?

A saying goes, "You always hurt the ones you love," and in some ways, this is true. A harsh comment from a loved one often carries a little more sting than one from a casual acquaintance. For this reason, it's extra important to keep your emotions under control during a conflict with a family member. You both have the power to hurt the other person with words, so choose them carefully. Be respectful when talking about a conflict with a family member. Remember, you'll be sitting across from each other at the dinner table tomorrow, so don't say anything you'll regret. Concentrate on making "I statements." If you find that you're spinning your wheels, you can always seek a mediator in another sibling or a parent. (Just try not to use the phrase, "I'm telling Mom!")

Try to work out conflicts with family members when you're not feeling emotionally charged.

COMMUNICATING AT WORK

When it comes to conflict management, the rules are different at work. Most workplaces have a chain of command. This means that you and other workers must do what your boss says, the boss must do what his or her boss says, and so on up the line. You might not be able to negotiate with a boss.

But that doesn't mean you can't resolve conflicts at work. Suppose you think your boss is showing favoritism toward other workers. Maybe you always get stuck with the worst shifts or maybe other workers are getting paid more for the same job. Ask your boss if you can talk in private. At the meeting, explain yourself clearly, without emotion. And, of course, listen. Your boss might have a perfectly good reason for what seems like favoritism.

Work conflicts can be tricky. You have to do what your boss says, but you can still use conflict resolution skills in the workplace.

Maybe you're the newest employee, and workers who have been on the job longer get the first choice of shifts. Or maybe the boss thinks you need to improve your performance in one area or another—and you won't get a raise until you do. *It's important to remember that in a work setting, such discussions are not among equals.* Your boss is in charge, and what he or she says goes. If you can't deal with that, it might be time to look for another job.

Conflicts with coworkers might be easier to handle. If you and a coworker are in conflict, try using the same conflict management strategies you'd use with any friend or family member. If you're not able to resolve the problem yourselves, you might want to bring in your boss as an arbitrator. But because of the chain of command at the workplace, you'll both have to stick with whatever decision the boss makes.

Coworkers must work as a team and keep conflicts to a minimum.

When you communicate by e-mail or text, others can't see your face or hear your voice. Without these important emotional cues, your message can be easily misunderstood.

COMMUNICATING ONLINE

Online conflict, including online bullying, is growing more and more common. Online, you might even end up in conflict with someone you've never met! Imagine that you take part in a message board for your favorite band. Maybe at some point, you and another poster get into an argument that grows more and more heated. How can you diffuse this tension?

The problem with online conflict is that we do all our online communication in writing. The other person doesn't get to see our facial expressions or hear our tone of voice. You might say something as a joke, but the other person thinks you're serious. On the other hand, a serious statement might be taken as sarcasm. *Without nonverbal cues, such as a smile or a wink, even an innocent comment can be taken as an insult*

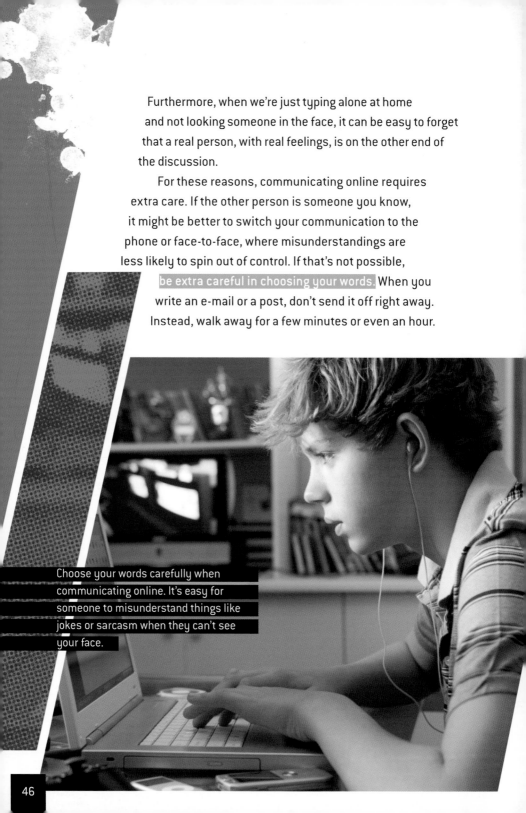

Furthermore, when we're just typing alone at home and not looking someone in the face, it can be easy to forget that a real person, with real feelings, is on the other end of the discussion.

For these reasons, communicating online requires extra care. If the other person is someone you know, it might be better to switch your communication to the phone or face-to-face, where misunderstandings are less likely to spin out of control. If that's not possible, be extra careful in choosing your words. When you write an e-mail or a post, don't send it off right away. Instead, walk away for a few minutes or even an hour.

Choose your words carefully when communicating online. It's easy for someone to misunderstand things like jokes or sarcasm when they can't see your face.

To really make sure you're understood, avoid electronic communication altogether. Meet for a talk over coffee.

Then come back and read it. On second read, you might realize that parts of your message could be hurtful or misunderstood. Then you can revise and edit the text to make a message that is constructive and not hurtful.

If an online situation does get out of hand and if someone starts sending you abusive and hateful messages, report the person to the site's administrator. The administrator might suspend or ban the abusive person from the site. If posts become threatening, tell a parent or another adult. You might even have to call law enforcement if you feel your safety is being threatened.

4 THE FINAL FRONTIER:
Resolution

Most games have a clear winner and loser. But with many conflicts, you can make sure that all people win—or at least get some of what they want.

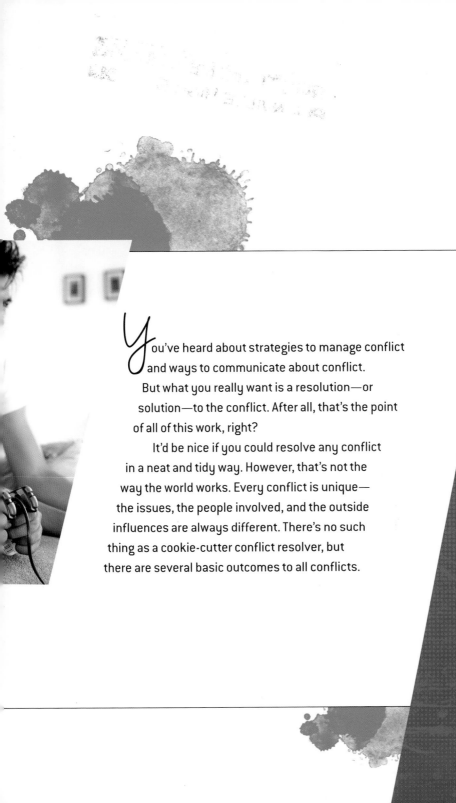

*Y*ou've heard about strategies to manage conflict and ways to communicate about conflict. But what you really want is a resolution—or solution—to the conflict. After all, that's the point of all of this work, right?

It'd be nice if you could resolve any conflict in a neat and tidy way. However, that's not the way the world works. Every conflict is unique— the issues, the people involved, and the outside influences are always different. There's no such thing as a cookie-cutter conflict resolver, but there are several basic outcomes to all conflicts.

WIN-WIN

The ultimate goal in conflict resolution is to find a solution in which each side gets what it wants—a win-win resolution. Let's step back to the New Year's Eve party from the beginning of this book. Your friend Alex has hurt your feelings by planning a New Year's party, knowing full well that you also planned to throw one. And you blew off a discussion that Alex had started about wanting to host next year's party. As it turns out, Alex is angry about that.

Does this conflict have a win-win resolution? It might, but first, you'll have to communicate and collaborate. Start by asking Alex to meet you somewhere to talk. Using "I statements," tell her that your feelings were hurt.

At first it might seem that a conflict has no resolution. But with some careful communication, you may find a solution that makes both of you happy.

Also listen attentively and patiently when she replies. When all the cards are on the table, it's time to start looking for a solution.

Maybe, in the course of talking to Alex, you discover that she really just wants to be involved in planning the party—no matter whose house it's at. Perhaps the two of you can work together (collaborate) to throw a single party. You'd both get to play host, and the party would be that much better because you'd work together. This would be a perfect win-win resolution.

A win-win solution is the best possible outcome in resolving a conflict. The tips in this book can help get you there!

MAKING PEACE PERSONAL

By Nafeesa Syeed

Dawn Kepler says that if it weren't for her son Jesse's best friend, Samir, she probably would not know any Muslims [people who practice the Islamic religion]. Samir's father, Ali Belkacem, from Algeria, describes himself as a liberal Muslim. The boy's mother, Lynne Haroun, is an American Christian. Kepler and her husband, Mark Snyder, are Jewish.

The couples' 11-year-old sons have been inseparable since preschool. "I would never just walk up to them and say, 'Tell me your life story,'" says Kepler. "But when you see them more, you start having more intimate conversations. How often do Muslims and Jews have repeated chances to interact?"

Both families say their varied faiths and cultural backgrounds are enriching. "Samir has attended [Jewish religious] services with them, and we've gone over during [the Jewish holiday of] Passover," says Belkacem. "There are so many similarities in the [Muslim and Jewish] traditions."

Kepler says: "For me, having Ali as a friend is a wonderful thing. If you really want to know about Judaism or Muslims, you have to turn to someone; you can't just read a book. I feel fortunate to have someone to open doors so I can see new things."

Those at the International Camp for Conflict Resolution know what Kepler means. Every summer, the New York-based non-profit group Seeds of Peace brings together young people from troubled regions around the world to interact with peers from different backgrounds and learn peacemaking skills. This year, more than 450 teens attended the camp in Maine. The U.S. host delegates are selected by Seeds of Peace; other campers are chosen by their governments.

Amy, 17, has been a member of the American delegation for two years. While growing up in a predominantly Jewish community in Chicago, IL, Amy says, she generally heard only the Israeli side of the Middle East conflict [between Israeli Jews and Palestinian Muslims]. Her first time at camp was the first time she had ever met a Muslim.

"You begin to coexist," she says. "When others tell of their personal struggles and (you) hear stories you can't ignore, you learn the enemy has a face. I left so many sessions in tears."

Last year, Amy befriended fellow camper Iman, 18, a Muslim of Lebanese descent. Iman, a native of Exeter, New Hampshire, says the three-week camp creates intense friendships that allow participants to learn about other cultures.

Though the camp does not focus specifically on religion, it does allow kids to be exposed to other faiths. For example, "Once they know a person likes P. Diddy like they do, they ask, 'What else is below this person? Can I ask more questions and probe them?'" says Rebecca Hankin, a Seeds of Peace spokeswoman. "They start asking why (he or she) keeps kosher [a Jewish dietary practice] or celebrates Ramadan [a Muslim holiday], and they find out more about the person."

But both Amy and Iman say their communities are hesitant about reaching out. Iman says she once told a Palestinian friend about a Jewish acquaintance, and the friend told her: "You can't do that. Don't talk to him."

Amy says, "People don't like the idea. Some people don't like Arab-Israeli relationships. (They) have a really hard time seeing there are two sides. They say, 'Your friends aren't real.'"

Though interfaith organizations can help initiate dialogue, Sarah Abalil [a Jewish woman married to a Muslim man] believes personal relationships are even more important. "It's ultimately not going to hinge on an Oslo accord [a 1993 peace treaty between Israel and Palestinians] or a treaty. Peace has to start in people's hearts—and that's what I'm proud to be a part of."

—*October 9, 2002*

WIN-LOSE

Wouldn't it be great if all conflicts could end with win-win resolutions? Of course it would. It'd also be cool if you could grow money on trees and learn to fly. In other words, this idea is pure fantasy. In the real world, win-win resolutions are rare.

That brings us to the next outcome—win-lose. In a win-lose resolution, one side (the winner) gets what he or she wants, while the other (the loser) doesn't.

Once again, let's look at the New Year's Eve party. You and Alex could manage the conflict using competition. You could both throw parties, competing against each other for guests. But what if almost everyone ends up going to Alex's party and yours is a dud? Classic win-lose.

Or maybe you decide to manage the conflict by accommodation. Instead of collaborating or competing, you just let Alex throw the party. In this case, you're sacrificing your own goals and giving up on the conflict. This is another win-lose scenario. It's good news for Alex but not so great for you.

Not all solutions are equal. In some cases, when one person gets what she wants, the other person loses out.

LOSE-LOSE

Win-lose might not sound terrific, but the situation could get worse. *In a lose-lose resolution, nobody gets what he or she wants.*

Let's go back to that competition scenario. Let's say that you and Alex each throw a party on New Year's Eve, and you each invite the same people. You also bad-mouth each other and try to make your friends feel guilty if they agree to go to the other party. Soon your friends are tired of both of you and your constant bickering. They decide to avoid the drama altogether and hang out in another friend's basement on New Year's Eve—and they don't bother telling either you or Alex of the change in plans. So when New Year's Eve comes around, both you and Alex end up sitting alone, with no guests at your parties. Yeah, that's lose-lose. It doesn't sound like a lot of fun, does it?

Some solutions leave neither party satisfied. This is called lose-lose.

CONFLICT IN THE COURTROOM

A criminal trial is a very formal kind of conflict. On one side are the prosecutors. These lawyers bring legal action against someone accused of a crime. The prosecutors want the accused person to be found guilty and punished for the crime. On the other side of the conflict is the defense. These lawyers work for the accused person. They hope the judge or jury hearing the case will find the person not guilty of the crime or will impose the minimum punishment if the person is found guilty.

In criminal cases, often a judge acts as an arbitrator, making a final ruling on the case. Sometimes a jury makes the final ruling. Often the end result of a criminal trial is win-lose. If the accused is found guilty and sent to jail, the prosecution is the winner and the defense is the loser. If the accused is found not guilty and set free, the defense has won and the prosecution has lost.

Prosecutors and defenders might also use compromise in the courtroom. Here's how it works. Suppose a man is accused of burglary. But he's a small-time crook. The prosecutors aren't that interested in him, but they really want to nail his boss, the leader of a burglary ring. The prosecutors might offer the defense a deal. They'll change the charge from burglary to attempted burglary, a lesser crime with a lighter sentence, if the accused man gives them information on his boss. This is a compromise that everyone can live with. If he's found guilty, the accused man will get a light sentence. The prosecutors, meanwhile, get information that might help them lock up the boss of the burglary ring.

COMPROMISE

Winning and losing are clear-cut outcomes, but some conflict resolutions aren't so clear-cut. Compromise is a form of resolution with no real "winners" and "losers." *When you compromise, you give up some things to gain others.* You get some—but not all—of what you want, and the same is true for those on the other side of the conflict.

Let's say that you and Alex talk about your conflict regarding the New Year's Eve party. You quickly realize that your goals are incompatible—you're both determined to throw a party at your own home and in your own way, and working together isn't an option. What about a compromise? Suppose you and Alex agree to take turns hosting the New Year's Eve party, alternating years. With this compromise, neither of you gets what you want, to throw every party, but you both get *something*—an agreement that you'll each get your turn. Neither of you will probably be fully satisfied with this resolution, but neither of you is shut out in the deal. Getting something is better than getting nothing, right? And just maybe reaching a compromise will help save your friendship. That's good for both of you.

Top skills for new hires

Here's what employers identified as the most important skills, along with what recent college graduates said they believe employers most value. (Respondents were asked to identify the two most important skills.)

■ Employers ■ Recent graduates

Teamwork
44%
38%

Critical thinking/reasoning
33%
37%

Oral/written communication
30%
37%

Source: Peter D. Hart Research Associates based on surveys of 305 business leaders and 510 recent college graduates Nov. 2-Dec. 5, 2006

By Karl Gelles, USA TODAY, 2007

Conflicts resolution skills are useful in the workplace. Managers want employees who know how to work as a team and to communicate well.

These girls are all smiles at a sleepover party. If they use conflict resolution skills, they'll keep the good times coming.

The next time you find yourself at odds with a friend, a classmate, a family member, or even a stranger, think back to what you've read here. Ask yourself what you can do to effectively manage the conflict. *Remember the power of communicating and listening.* You might be surprised how far these skills will take you.

Of course, there's no secret weapon for managing all conflicts. No one tactic will make all conflicts go away, and of the tactics you've learned, not all will work in every situation. You can't always find a win-win resolution.

Sometimes you'll clash with someone who won't be willing to communicate or compromise. The best strategies in the world won't help you then. Other times, you may go head-to-head with a large organization or a corporation. In that situation, you might not be able to resolve your conflict by talking to a single person. You might have to talk to several customer service representatives or managers. You might even have to fill out forms or write letters to resolve your conflict. But even then, the tips you've learned in this book will help you communicate.

REMEMBER THESE TIPS:

Keep Emotions in Check

Some people react to conflict with anger, fear, or sadness, but these emotions can cloud your thinking. They can make you say things you wouldn't say in a clearer state of mind. Before discussing a conflict, try to get yourself in a calm, unemotional state. Try some simple meditation if you need it.

Listen!

Nobody likes to be lectured. If you're talking over a conflict, listening is just as important as talking (probably *more* important!). Let the other person know that you understand what he or she is saying.

Avoid the Blame Game

No matter how mad you might be, avoid placing blame for the conflict. Use sentences that begin with / to soften your message. You'll find that people respond a lot better to "I statements" than to "you statements."

Work as a Team

If you're in a conflict with someone, that person might not feel like a teammate. But in fact, he or she is your teammate in working together to resolve the conflict. Treat the other person with respect. Communicate openly and try to find a resolution that everyone can live with.

GLOSSARY

ACCOMMODATION: a conflict management strategy in which one party in a dispute gives in to the desires of the other party

ARBITRATION: a process in which a third, neutral person hears both sides of a dispute and comes up with a resolution, which the disputing parties must abide by

COLLABORATION: a conflict management strategy in which the people in conflict come together to find a resolution that makes everyone happy

COMPETITION: the process of striving against rivals for a prize, a position, or an honor. Competition can be the root of some conflicts. Some conflicts can be resolved using competition.

COMPROMISE: a conflict management strategy in which each side gets some, but not all, of what it wants

CONFLICT: a disagreement or dispute between two or more people or groups, usually with opposing goals

CONFLICT MANAGEMENT: handling conflict in a positive way

CONFLICT RESOLUTION: the outcome of a conflict

EMPATHY: the ability to understand the thoughts and feelings of others

GHOST CONFLICT: a minor or trivial conflict that people focus on to avoid dealing with a more serious conflict

GRIDLOCK: a state, usually in politics, in which nothing gets done because neither side is willing to compromise

MEDIATION: a process in which a third, neutral person helps people solve a dispute. A mediator only helps people communicate but does not have authority to resolve the conflict.

MEDITATION: a process in which an individual focuses his or her thoughts inward, toward a calm and peaceful state

NEGOTIATION: the process of building a compromise, where each side makes proposals and gives a little ground, trying to meet in the middle

SELECTED BIBLIOGRAPHY

Dana, Daniel. *Conflict Resolution: Mediation Tools for Everyday Worklife*. New York: McGraw-Hill, 2001.

Moore, Christopher W. *The Mediation Process: Practical Strategies for Resolving Conflict*. San Francisco: Jossey-Bass, 2003.

Ramsbotham, Oliver, Tom Woodhouse, and Hugh Miall. *Contemporary Conflict Resolution: The Prevention, Management and Transformation of Deadly Conflicts*. Malden, MA: Polity, 2005.

Schellenberg, James A. *Conflict Resolution: Theory, Research, and Practice*. Albany: State University of New York Press, 1996.

Stitt, Allan. *Mediation: A Practical Guide*. Portland, OR: Cavendish, 2004.

Ursiny, Tim. *The Coward's Guide to Conflict: Empowering Solutions for Those Who Would Rather Run Than Fight*. Naperville, IL: Sourcebooks, 2003.

Weeks, Dudley. *The Eight Essential Steps to Conflict Resolution: Preserving Relationships at Work, at Home, and in the Community*. Los Angeles: Jeremy P. Tarcher, 1992.

Wood, Julia. *Interpersonal Communication: Everyday Encounters*. Boston: Wadsworth Cengage, 2008.

FOR MORE INFORMATION

Carlson, Dale Bick. *Talk: Teen Art of Communication*. Madison, CT: Bick Publishing House, 2006.
This book will teach you more about effective communication and how to express your thoughts and feelings to others.

Casey, Carolyn. *Conflict Resolution: The Win-Win Situation*. Berkeley Heights, NJ: Enslow Publishers, 2001.
Casey walks readers through conflict management strategies and discusses how to overcome roadblocks to conflict resolution.

Conflict Resolution Fact Sheet for Teens
http://www.csgv.ca/counselor/assets/Conflict%20Resolution%20Fact%20 Sheet%20for%20Teens.pdf
The National Youth Violence Prevention Resource Center has put together this handy reference for teens dealing with conflict.

Gallagher, Jim, and Dorothy Kavanaugh. *A Guys' Guide to Conflict/A Girls' Guide to Conflict*. Berkeley Heights, NJ: Enslow, 2008.
This book includes separate guides for guys and girls on dealing with issues such as bullying and gossip.

Golus, Carrie. *Take a Stand! What You Can Do about Bullying*. Minneapolis: Lerner Publications Company, 2009. Bullying is a problem for many kids and teens. The author goes over the causes of bullying and suggests ways to deal with the conflict.

HowStuffWorks—Five Things to Know: Family Fights
http://tlc.howstuffworks.com/family/5-things-to-know-family-fights.htm
Check out this site to read about dealing with conflicts within the family. Learn about stress, staying calm, communicating, and more.

KidsHealth—Dealing with Bullying
http://kidshealth.org/teen/your_mind/problems/bullies.html
This site provides in-depth information on the problem of bullying. It gives advice to those being bullied, as well as to those doing the bullying, on how to resolve conflicts.

Making Peace: Tips on Conflict Management
http://www.ncpc.org/cms/cms-upload/ncpc/files/making_peace.pdf
This printable brochure from the National Crime Prevention Council will help
teens remember the steps for working out a conflict and keeping the peace.

Markovics, Joyce. *Relationship Smarts: How to Navigate Dating, Friendship,
Family Relationships, and More*. Minneapolis: Twenty-First Century Books,
2012.
This title from the Teen Wise series will help kids build better relationships,
whether with friends, family members, or love interests.

McCollum, Sean. *Managing Conflict Resolution*. New York: Chelsea House,
2009. Learn more about what conflict is, where and why it happens, and
strategies for dealing with it.

Peer Mediation
http://www.peermediation.org
Peer mediation is a growing trend in both schools and the business world.
Read all about it at this site, and learn about how and why it works.

Six Steps for Resolving Conflicts
http://www.learningpeace.com/pages/LP_04.htm
Naomi Drew, an expert in conflict resolution, offers a six-step program for
resolving conflicts. Check it out and see if it works for you!

Sommers, Michael A. *Great Interpersonal Skills*. New York: Rosen, 2008.
Sommers explains effective ways to interact with others in a variety of
situations, from team building to conflict resolution.

LERNER

SOURCE™

Expand learning beyond the printed book. Download free, complementary
educational resources for this book from our website, www.lerneresource.com.

INDEX

accommodation, 20, 24–25, 54
arbitration, 20, 26, 44, 56

bullying, 16, 31, 38–39, 45

collaboration, 20, 30, 50–51
communication, 11, 32–34, 36–37, 38, 40–43, 45–47, 49–50, 57, 58–59
competition, 9, 20–21, 54–55
compromise, 20, 22, 24, 26, 56–57, 59
conflicting values, 8, 10, 11, 12
conflict resolution (definition), 8

emotions, 13–14, 35, 38, 40–43, 45, 59

ghost conflicts, 34

internal conflict, 8
"I statements," 37, 42, 50, 59

mediation, 20, 26, 31, 42

negotiation, 22–23

online conflict, 45–47

peer mediator, 31

time-out, 35
triggering event, 13

ABOUT THE AUTHOR

Matt Doeden has written and edited hundreds of nonfiction books. Lots of them are on high-interest topics such as cars, sports, and airplanes. He also writes and edits books about geography, science, and even math.